Donovan

by Iain Gray

Lang**Syne**

PUBLISHING

WRITING *to* REMEMBER

Office 5, Vineyard Business Centre,
Pathhead, Midlothian EH37 5XP
Tel: 01875 321 203 Fax: 01875 321 233
E-mail: info@lang-syne.co.uk
www.langsyneshop.co.uk

Design by Dorothy Meikle
Printed by Hay Nisbet Press, Glasgow
© Lang Syne Publishers Ltd 2009

ISBN 978-1-85217-310-4

Donovan

MOTTO:
God aiding against enemies.

CREST:
A falcon.

NAME variations include:
Ó Donamháin (*Gaelic*)
Ó Donnabháin (*Gaelic*)
O'Donovan
Donavan
Donavon
Donevan
Donnavan
Donnavon
Donnovan

Chapter one:
Origins of Irish surnames

According to an old saying, there are two types of Irish – those who actually are Irish and those who wish they were.

This sentiment is only one example of the allure that the high romance and drama of the proud nation's history holds for thousands of people scattered across the world today.

It's a sad fact, however, that the vast majority of Irish surnames are found far beyond Irish shores, rather than on the Emerald Isle itself.

The population stood at around eight million souls in 1841, but today it stands at fewer than six million.

This is mainly a tragic consequence of the potato famine, also known as the Great Hunger, which devastated Ireland between 1845 and 1849.

The Irish peasantry had become almost wholly reliant for basic sustenance on the potato, first introduced from the Americas in the seventeenth century.

When the crop was hit by a blight, at least 800,000 people starved to death while an estimated two million others were forced to seek a new life far from their native shores – particularly in America, Canada, and Australia.

The effects of the potato blight continued until about 1851, by which time a firm pattern of emigration had become established.

Ireland's loss, however, was to the gain of the countries in which the immigrants settled, contributing enormously, as their descendants do today, to the well being of the nations in which their forefathers settled.

But those who were forced through dire circumstance to establish a new life in foreign parts never forgot their roots, or the proud heritage and traditions of the land that gave them birth.

Nor do their descendants.

It is a heritage that is inextricably bound up in the colourful variety of Irish names themselves – and the origin and history of these names forms an integral part of the vibrant drama that is the nation's history, one of both glorious fortune and tragic misfortune.

This history is well documented, and one of the most important and fascinating of the earliest sources are *The Annals of the Four Masters*, compiled between 1632 and 1636 by four friars at the Franciscan Monastery in County Donegal.

Compiled from earlier sources, and purporting to go back to the Biblical Deluge, much of the material takes in the mythological origins and history of Ireland and the Irish.

This includes tales of successive waves of invaders and settlers such as the Fomorians, the Partholonians, the Nemedians, the Fir Bolgs, the Tuatha De Danann, and the Laigain.

Of particular interest are the *Milesian Genealogies*,

because the majority of Irish clans today claim a descent from either Heremon, Ir, or Heber – three of the sons of Milesius, a king of what is now modern day Spain.

These sons invaded Ireland in the second millennium B.C, apparently in fulfilment of a mysterious prophecy received by their father.

This Milesian lineage is said to have ruled Ireland for nearly 3,000 years, until the island came under the sway of England's King Henry II in 1171 following what is known as the Cambro-Norman invasion.

This is an important date not only in Irish history in general, but for the effect the invasion subsequently had for Irish surnames.

'Cambro' comes from the Welsh, and 'Cambro-Norman' describes those Welsh knights of Norman origin who invaded Ireland.

But they were invaders who stayed, inter-marrying with the native Irish population and founding their own proud dynasties that bore Cambro-Norman names such as Archer, Barbour, Brannagh, Fitzgerald, Fitzgibbon, Fleming, Joyce, Plunkett, and Walsh – to name only a few.

These 'Cambro-Norman' surnames that still flourish throughout the world today form one of the three main categories in which Irish names can be placed – those of Gaelic-Irish, Cambro-Norman, and Anglo-Irish.

Previous to the Cambro-Norman invasion of the twelfth century, and throughout the earlier invasions and settlement of those wild bands of sea rovers known as the Vikings in the eighth and ninth centuries, the population of the island was relatively small, and it was normal for a person to be identified through the use of only a forename.

But as population gradually increased and there were many more people with the same forename, surnames were adopted to distinguish one person, or one community, from another.

Individuals identified themselves with their own particular tribe, or 'tuath', and this tribe – that also became known as a clann, or clan – took its name from some distinguished ancestor who had founded the clan.

The Gaelic-Irish form of the name Kelly, for example, is Ó Ceallaigh, or O'Kelly, indicating descent from an original 'Ceallaigh', with the 'O' denoting 'grandson of.' The name was later anglicised to Kelly.

The prefix 'Mac' or 'Mc', meanwhile, as with the clans of the Scottish Highlands, denotes 'son of.'

Although the Irish clans had much in common with their Scottish counterparts, one important difference lies in what are known as 'septs', or branches, of the clan.

Septs of Scottish clans were groups who often bore an entirely different name from the clan name but were under the clan's protection.

In Ireland, septs were groups that shared the same name and who could be found scattered throughout the four provinces of Ulster, Leinster, Munster, and Connacht.

The 'golden age' of the Gaelic-Irish clans, infused as their veins were with the blood of Celts, pre-dates the Viking invasions of the eighth and ninth centuries and the Norman invasion of the twelfth century, and the sacred heart of the country was the Hill of Tara, near the River Boyne, in County Meath.

Known in Gaelic as 'Teamhar na Rí', or Hill of Kings, it was the royal seat of the 'Ard Rí Éireann', or High King of Ireland, to whom the petty kings, or chieftains, from the island's provinces were ultimately subordinate.

It was on the Hill of Tara, beside a stone pillar known as the Irish 'Lia Fáil', or Stone of Destiny, that the High Kings were inaugurated and, according to legend, this stone would emit a piercing screech that could be heard all over Ireland when touched by the hand of the rightful king.

The Hill of Tara is today one of the island's main tourist attractions.

Opposition to English rule over Ireland, established in the wake of the Cambro-Norman invasion, broke out frequently and the harsh solution adopted by the powerful forces of the Crown was to forcibly evict the native Irish from their lands.

These lands were then granted to Protestant colonists, or 'planters', from Britain.

Many of these colonists, ironically, came from Scotland and were the descendants of the original 'Scotti', or 'Scots', who gave their name to Scotland after migrating there in the fifth century A.D., from the north of Ireland.

Colonisation entailed harsh penal laws being imposed on the majority of the native Irish population, stripping them practically of all of their rights.

The Crown's main bastion in Ireland was Dublin and its environs, known as the Pale, and it was the dispossessed peasantry who lived outside this Pale, desperately striving to eke out a meagre living.

It was this that gave rise to the modern-day expression of someone or something being 'beyond the pale'.

Attempts were made to stamp out all aspects of the ancient Gaelic-Irish culture, to the extent that even to bear a Gaelic-Irish name was to invite discrimination.

This is why many Gaelic-Irish names were anglicised with, for example, and noted above, Ó Ceallaigh, or O'Kelly, being anglicised to Kelly.

Succeeding centuries have seen strong revivals of Gaelic-Irish consciousness, however, and this has led to many families reverting back to the original form of their name, while the language itself is frequently found on the fluent tongues of an estimated 90,000 to 145,000 of the island's population.

Ireland's turbulent history of religious and political strife is one that lasted well into the twentieth century, a landmark century that saw the partition of the island into the twenty-six counties of the independent Republic of

Ireland, or Eire, and the six counties of Northern Ireland, or Ulster.

Dublin, originally founded by Vikings, is now a vibrant and truly cosmopolitan city while the proud city of Belfast is one of the jewels in the crown of Ulster.

It was Saint Patrick who first brought the light of Christianity to Ireland in the fifth century A.D.

Interpretations of this Christian message have varied over the centuries, often leading to bitter sectarian conflict – but the many intricately sculpted Celtic Crosses found all over the island are symbolic of a unity that crosses the sectarian divide.

It is an image that fuses the 'old gods' of the Celts with Christianity.

All the signs from the early years of this new millennium indicate that sectarian strife may soon become a thing of the past – with the Irish and their many kinsfolk across the world, be they Protestant or Catholic, finding common purpose in the rich tapestry of their shared heritage.

Chapter two:

The brown-haired chiefs

The southwestern Irish province of Munster is the original homeland of bearers of the proud name of Donovan, and it was here that for centuries they were closely involved in some of the most pivotal episodes in the island's turbulent history.

The Gaelic-Irish form of the name is Ó Donamháin, or Ó Donnabháin, thought to indicate 'descendant of the brown-haired chief', and it was these 'brown-haired chiefs' and their kinsfolk who were first found in the southern reaches of present day Co. Limerick in the area of Bruree, on the banks of the River Maigue.

Members of the tribal grouping known as the Uí Fidhgheinte, the majority of the clan relocated southwards towards the end of the twelfth century to the area of present day West Cork, where they flourished for centuries in the baronies of West and East Carbery.

Other septs of Donovans were still to be found, and found to this day, in the counties of Wexford, Waterford, and Kilkenny.

The senior line of the family is known as the Clan Cathail, or Clan Cathal – a line that, along with Clan Lochlain, eventually fused its fortunes with those of the Ó Donamháins of Corca Laidhe.

The Chief of the Name today, recognised as such through his descent from Clan Cathail, is known as 'The O'Donovan.'

The Donovan lineage is truly illustrious, descended as they are from Olioll Flann-Beag who, in turn, was of the celebrated royal line of the Milesian monarchs of Ireland.

This was through one of the sons of Milesius, a king of what is now modern day Spain, and who had planned to invade Ireland in fulfilment of a mysterious Druidic prophecy.

Milesius died before he could launch his invasion across the sea to Ireland, but eight sons who included Amergin, Hebor, Ir, and Heremon undertook the task.

Five sons, including Ir, were killed in battle against the Tuatha-De-Danann shortly after battling their way from the shoreline to the soil of Ireland.

This was soil, however, that Ir's offspring and the offspring of his brothers Heber and Heremon were destined to hold for centuries as warrior kings.

According to the Milesian genealogies, Heremon and Heber began to rule the land they had conquered from about 1699 B.C.

The Donovans, or O'Donovans, trace a descent back to Heber, who was killed by Heremon in a quarrel over territory.

The clan, in common with the equally illustrious Clan O'Brien, were also of the famed Race of Cas, also known as the DalgCais, or Dalcassians – named from the legendary

Cormac Cas, the early to mid-third century chieftain of Munster who was renowned for his remarkable courage, strength, and dexterity.

It was he who inflicted a celebrated defeat on the men of the province of Leinster in a battle fought near present day Wexford, but was killed in battle in 254 A.D. at Dun-tri-Liag, or the Fort of the Stone Slabs, known today as Duntrileague, in Co. Limerick.

His deathblow, according to the ancient annals, came from the spear of the Leinster king known rather colourfully as Eochy of the Red Eyebrows.

Members of the Dalcassian sept often found themselves at odds with one another, and this was illustrated in dramatic fashion in 977 A.D. in the form of an O'Donovan chieftain who sided with Ivor, a King of the Vikings of Limerick, in battle against one of Ireland's greatest warrior kings.

This was no less a figure than Brian Bóruma mac Cénnetig, a younger son of Cennetig, king of Thomond, in the northern reaches of Munster, born in about 926 A.D. and better known as Brian Boru.

How O'Donovan came to be embroiled in battle against fellow members of the Dalcassian sept can be found in the complex and vicious inter-clan rivalries of the time.

Mahon, a brother of Brian Boru, and Maolmoradh, of the dynastic line known as the Eugenian, had been locked in bitter and bloody dispute over the prize of the kingship of Munster.

In a bid to resolve the impasse, leading ecclesiastics proposed that both contenders for the throne should attempt to settle their differences peacefully by meeting at the neutral territory of the O'Donovan chieftain.

But dark treachery was in the air.

Maolmoradh arrived at O'Donovan's stronghold in present-day Co. Kerry and managed to bribe him into supporting his cause.

Accompanied by only twelve of his followers, Mahon arrived later at the O'Donovan stronghold – only to be pounced upon through the connivance of O'Donovan and later, in the words of the annals 'basely murdered.'

Maolmoradh was by default duly proclaimed King of Munster, and O'Donovan rewarded with the grant of lands.

This was during a period known in Ireland known as the Viking Tyranny, a period that had commenced in the closing years of the eighth century A.D. when their sinister longboats first appeared off Irish shores.

The monastery of St. Patrick's Island, near Skerries in present day Co. Dublin was looted and burned to the ground, and raids continued along the coastline until they made their first forays inland in 836 A.D., while a year later a Viking fleet of 60 vessels sailed into the River Boyne.

An indication of the terror they brought can be found in one contemporary account of their depredations and desecrations.

It lamented how 'the pagans desecrated the sanctuaries

of God, and poured out the blood of saints upon the altar, laid waste the house of our hope, trampled on the bodies of saints in the temple of God, like dung in the street.'

By 841 A.D. the Vikings, or Ostmen as they were also known, had established a number of strongholds on the island, but their raids began to ease off before returning with a terrifying and bloody vengeance in about 914 A.D.

By 977 A.D the O'Donovan chieftain had found himself in alliance with Ivor, a King of Vikings who had established themselves in Limerick, through his marriage to his daughter.

They were defeated in battle by Brian Boru and his Dalcassian knights and shortly afterwards, the O'Donovan chieftain was killed at the battle of Croma.

Some sources say he was slain at the hands of Donchuan, a nephew of Brian Boru, while other sources assert it was at the hands of Boru himself.

It was this O'Donovan chieftain's son, Cathail, or Cathal, who is recognised as having been the first to assume the Donovan surname and who found the Donovan sept of Clan Cathail.

With his battle-hardened warriors known as the Dalcassian knights at his side, Brian Boru had by 1002 A.D. achieved the prize of the High Kingship of Ireland – but there were still rival chieftains, and not least the Vikings, to deal with.

Resenting Boru's High Kingship, a number of

chieftains, particularly those of the province of Leinster, found common cause with the Ostmen, and the two sides met in final and bloody confrontation at the battle of Clontarf, four miles north of Dublin, on Good Friday 1014.

Among Boru's supporters was Amhailgadh O'Donovan, Cathail's son, and who fought with great valour in a cavalry division commanded by Boru's son-in-law, Cián, Prince of Kinalmeaky.

Boru proved victorious, but the annals speak of great slaughter on the day, with the dead piled high on the field of battle, while among the many dead were Brian Boru's three sons.

The great warrior king himself was killed by a party of fleeing Vikings, but not before felling most of them with his mighty two-handed sword.

Amhailgadh O'Donovan, who survived the battle, had meanwhile more than atoned for the treachery of his grandfather against the Dalcassian sept.

Chapter three:

Freedom's struggle

Less than 200 years after Brian Boru's great victory over the Vikings at the battle of Clontarf, aided by warriors including Amhailgadh O'Donovan, the island was devastated by a fresh wave of invaders.

These were battle-hardened and ambitious Norman knights who crossed the Irish Sea from Bristol, on the coastline of Wales, in 1169.

Their onslaught on the island was swift and deadly, and by 1175 English dominion over Ireland was ratified through the Treaty of Windsor under the terms of which native Irish chieftains were allowed to rule territory unoccupied by the Normans in the role of vassals of the English monarch.

Further waves of settlers poured into the Ireland in the wake of the English Crown's policy of settling, or 'planting' loyal Protestants on Irish land.

This policy had started during the reign from 1491 to 1547 of Henry VIII, whose Reformation effectively outlawed the established Roman Catholic faith throughout his dominions.

This settlement of loyal Protestants in Ireland, from both England and Scotland, continued throughout the subsequent reigns of Elizabeth I, James I (James VI of Scotland), and Charles I.

Among the many victims of this blatant land-grabbing policy were the Donovans, who lost much of their territories and the stronghold of the castle of Crom, in Co. Limerick, to the powerful forces of the Anglo-Norman Maurice Fitzgerald, who became Lord Justice of Ireland in 1229.

The Fitzgerald success in defeating the Donovans is commemorated to this day in their triumphant family motto of 'Crom-a-boo', indicting 'victory at Crom.'

By this stage in the Donovan family fortunes most of the sept had found themselves pushed inexorably towards the area of present day West Cork – and even here they had to contend with not only the encroachment of settlers from the English and Scottish mainlands, but also destructive inter-clan rivalries.

By the late sixteenth century the heir to the precarious chieftainship of the Donovans was Donal Na-g-Crolceainn, or Donal of the Hides.

His rather unusual name came from the fact that as a child, his mother had to wrap and conceal him in a cowhide to hide him from ambitious and ruthless claimants to the Donovan chieftainship.

But he and his mother found an ally in the powerful Clan McCarthy who, in keeping with their ancient traditions, presented him with the 'white wand' of the McCarthys – indicating that they recognised him as the rightful Donovan chieftain.

One of his descendants, Donal O'Donovan, described

by contemporary sources as 'distinguished both in peace and war, admired by his friends and respected by his enemies', became embroiled in the terrible events that erupted on the island in 1641.

It was in this year that many native Irish clans such as the Donovans erupted in a fury of discontent over the policy of plantation.

Hundreds of Protestant settlers were driven from their lands to seek refuge where they could, while eight years later vengeance arrived in the form of the Cromwellian invasion of the island.

Donal O'Donovan, who had taken a leading role in the rebellion against English rule, had sided with the Earl of Castlehaven and been responsible in 1645 for the capture of the bastions of Rostellan, Connagh, and Milton castles.

In the aftermath of the Cromwellian victory the island was held in a grip of iron, allowing the implementation of what in modern day terms would be described as a policy of ethnic cleansing.

Cromwell's troopers were given free rein to hunt down and kill priests, while what remained of Catholic estates such as those of the Donovans were confiscated.

An edict was also issued stating that any native Irish found east of the River Shannon after May 1, 1654 faced either summary execution or transportation to the West Indies.

By 1652 Donal O'Donovan had been stripped of large

tracts of his territory, much of which passed into the ownership of Cromwell's troopers and land speculators.

Following the Restoration of the Stuart monarch Charles II to the throne in 1660, Donal O'Donovan's son, also called Donal, petitioned the king for the return of his family's lands – but received only a small portion of the original estates.

Still loyal to the Stuart cause, Donal also played a key role in Ireland in the aftermath of what is known as the Glorious Revolution.

This involved the flight into exile in 1688 of James II and the accession to the throne of the Protestant William of Orange and his wife Mary.

Followers of James were known as Jacobites, and Donal O'Donovan fought for the cause in his role as a Colonel in a Regiment of Foot and as deputy governor of Charlesfort.

But the cause was doomed, and Jacobite defeat was finally ratified through the signing of the Treaty of Limerick in 1691; Donal died twelve years later.

In common with other Irish Catholic families, some Donovans converted to the Protestant faith in a bid to retain their estates and privileges.

Many prospered in the service of the state, including Richard O'Donovan, who was born in 1764 and became a Colonel in the Enniskillen Dragoons and later achieved the rank of General in the British Army.

Others fought for the cause of Ireland's freedom from

British rule following the union of the English and Irish parliaments in 1800.

One leading Republican was Jeremiah O'Donovan Rossa, born in 1831 in Rosscarbery, Co. Cork, and who founded the Phoenix National and Literary Society.

The aim of the society was 'the liberation of Ireland by force of arms' and it eventually merged with the Irish Republican Brotherhood (IRB).

Sentenced to life imprisonment in 1865 for his part in plotting a rising against British rule, he was later released as part of an amnesty and allowed to leave Ireland for America.

It was from here, in New York, that he orchestrated a bombing campaign of English cities, while the British government fought in vain for his extradition.

He died in 1915, but his body was returned for burial in Dublin's Glasnevin Cemetery, where the Republican leader Patrick Pearse delivered a celebrated graveside oration.

There is a monument to O'Donovan Rossa in Dublin's St. Stephen's Green.

Chapter four:

On the world stage

Donovans and their namesakes the O'Donovans have excelled at an international level in a rich variety of pursuits.

Born in 1968 in Malvern, Melbourne, **Jason Donovan** is the Australian singer and actor whose first television appearance was at the tender age of 11 in the series *Skyways*.

But it was as one of the stars in the 1980s, beside the actress and singer Kylie Minogue, of the popular television soap *Neighbours* that he achieved international fame.

A teen idol, he went on to record a string of hit songs, including the 1988 duet with Kylie Minogue, *Especially for You*.

Films he has appeared in include the 1990 *Blood Oath*, while in recent years he has turned his talents to working as the leading man in stage musicals – most notably *Joseph and the Amazing Technicolour Dreamcoat*.

Acting may well have been in his blood from birth, because his father **Terry Donovan** is one of Australia's most popular television actors.

Born in 1942 in England and later immigrating to Australia, he has had roles in drama series that include *Cop Show*, *Prisoner*, *Sons and Daughters* and, in common with his son, *Neighbours*.

Also on the stage **Mark Donovan**, born in 1968 in Aberdare, Wales, is the Welsh character actor rather scarily best known for his grotesque roles in films and television shows such as the 2004 *Shaun of the Dead*, *Murder Investigation Team*, *Black Books*, *Dr. Who*, and the 2008 *In Bruges*.

Born in 1971 in Poughkeepsie, New York, **Elisha Donovan** is the American actress who played Maureen Cavanaugh in the television sitcom *Sabrina, the Teenage Witch* and whose film roles include *A Night at the Roxbury*.

Tate Donovan, born in 1963 in New York City, is the American television and film actor and director whose film roles include the 1990 *Memphis Belle* and who has appeared in episodes of *Friends* and *The O.C.*

Born in 1954, **Paul Donovan** is the Canadian television and film writer, producer, and director who created the popular science fiction series *LEXX*.

A co-founder along with his brother Michael of Salter Street Films, he was involved in the production of the 2000 Michael Moore documentary *Bowling for Columbine* – winner of an Academy Award for Best Documentary Feature.

In the world of music Donovan Phillips Leitch, born in 1946 in the Maryhill area of Glasgow, is the Scottish singer, songwriter and guitarist better known simply as **Donovan**.

Moving with his family to Hatfield, in England, when he was aged 10, he later became involved in the British folk music scene – influenced by his parents' interest in the traditional folk music of both his native Scotland and England.

Following a short spell at art school he took to the road with his guitar, eking out a meagre existence playing small clubs and busking.

He was aged only 20 when offered a music management and publishing contract in 1964, and a string of hits that blended folk with jazz, pop, and psychedelic influences rapidly followed.

These included *Colours*, *Sunshine Superman*, *Season of the Witch*, *Mellow Yellow*, *There is a Mountain*, and *Hurdy Gurdy Man*.

Still recording and touring, he is now resident in the United States.

His son is the musician and actor **Donovan Leitch Jnr.**, born in England in 1968 and whose mother is the former model Enid Stulberger.

His mother and father separated when he was aged three, and he moved with his mother to the United States where he later became a founding member along with Jason Nesmith, son of the Monkee's Mike Nesmith, of the group Nancy Boy.

Turning to acting, he has become involved in films that include *I Shot Andy Warhol*, while his sister is the actress Iona Skye.

From the world of music to the dark and sinister world

of warfare and spies, Major General William Donovan was the American lawyer, soldier and intelligence officer better known as **Wild Bill Donovan**, and who was born in 1883 in Buffalo, New York.

He was responsible during the First World War for organising and leading the 69th New York Volunteers, more famously known as The Fighting 69th.

Promoted to Colonel, he received the Distinguished Service Cross and three Purple Hearts.

Before America's entry into the Second World War he worked as a Wall Street lawyer, but in 1941 he was given responsibility for the creation of America's Office of Strategic Services (OSS), whose later remit was to carry out espionage and acts of sabotage in occupied Europe and parts of Japanese occupied Asia.

The OSS was the forerunner of today's Central Intelligence Agency (CIA), and that is why Donovan, who was promoted to Major General at the end of the war, is known as the 'father' of the CIA.

Buried in Washington's Arlington National Cemetery, Donovan was the recipient of a host of honours that included an honorary British knighthood, America's Distinguished Service Medal, and membership of the Military Intelligence Hall of Fame.

When he died in 1959 President Dwight D. Eisenhower described him as 'The Last Hero'.

Also on the field of battle **Edmund O'Donovan**, born

in 1844 in Dublin, was the nineteenth century war correspondent for newspapers that included the *London Daily News* and who was killed in 1883 in an ill-fated British military expedition to the Sudan.

In the world of business Michael O'Donovan, better known as **Val O'Donovan**, was the Irish electrical engineering genius and businessman who was born in 1936 in Cork.

He immigrated with his family to Canada in 1963 to take up a post with an international communications company, but by less than ten years later he had founded his own satellite communication company, ComDev.

O'Donovan, who died in 2005, served as Chancellor of the University of Waterloo from 1997 to 2003, the same year in which he was made a Member of the Order of Canada, the nation's highest civilian honour.

Donovans have also excelled, and continue to excel, in the highly competitive world of sport.

Born in 1961 in Ridgewood, New Jersey, **Anne Donovan** is one of the leading figures in American Women's Basketball, both as a player and a coach.

A member of the Basketball Hall of Fame and a gold medal winner for the U.S. Women's Team at the 1984 and 1988 Olympics, she was appointed head coach for the team for the 2008 Olympics in Beijing, China.

In baseball **Dick Donovan**, born in 1927 in Boston and who died in 1977, was the starting pitcher in Major League

Baseball who played for teams that included the Boston Braves and Cleveland Indians, while **Patsy Donovan** was the Irish-American right fielder and manager who was born in 1865 in Queenstown, Co. Cork.

He started playing the game in 1886 with the Lawrence, Massachusetts, team, later playing for several teams from 1890 to 1907, including the Pittsburgh Pirates.

Donovan, who died in 1953, ended his career by coaching High School baseball – and among those he coached was the then future 41st President of the United States, George W. Bush.

In contemporary soccer **Landon Donovan**, born in 1982 in Redlands, California, is the professional player who, at the time of writing, plays for the famed Los Angeles Galaxy, and is the all-time leading scorer for the United States' men's national team.

In professional ice hockey Shean Donovan, born in 1975 in Timmins, Ontario is the talented right-winger who, at the time of writing, plays for the Ottawa Senators.

From sport to the creative world of photography, **Terence Donovan** was the British photographer and film director who was born in the east end of London in 1936.

He became famous in the 1960s for his fashion photography and, along with fellow British photographer David Bailey, his name became synonymous with the London of the 'Swinging Sixties.'

Towards the end of his career he became involved in

documentaries and music videos. He committed suicide in 1996.

His daughter is the actress, television presenter and writer **Daisy Donovan**, born in 1975 in Brooklyn, New York.

Known for her appearances on satirical British television shows such as *The Eleven O'Clock Show*, she has also appeared in films such as the 2007 *Death at a Funeral* and the 2008 *Wild Child*.

Her mother is **Diana Donovan**, chairwoman at the time of writing of the English National Ballet School, while her half-brother **Dan Donovan**, born in 1962, is famed as the keyboard player with the band *Big Audio Dynamite*.

In the world of art **William O'Donovan**, born in 1844 in Preston County, Virginia, and who died in 1920, was the American sculptor and associate of the National Academy of Design whose many works include the statues of Lincoln and Grant in Brooklyn's Grand Army Plaza.

Donovans and their namesakes the O'Donovans have also produced some of Ireland's greatest scholars.

Born in Kilkenny in 1809, **John O'Donovan** was responsible for the compilation of a record of Ireland's place names after visiting every parish on the island in his capacity as an employee of the Irish Record Office's ordnance survey department.

O'Donovan, who died in 1861, was also for a time professor of Celtic studies at Queen's College, Belfast.

Born in Cork in 1903, **Michael O'Donovan** was the Irish writer, historian and folklorist whose works included a six-volume translation of that valuable treasure trove of historical information known as *The Annals of the Four Masters*.

Along with his brother-in-law and fellow scholar Eugene O'Curry, he was also responsible for proposing the *Dictionary of the Irish Language* – a monumental work that the Royal Irish Academy commenced in 1913 and finally completed in 1976.

In the age of the amateur gentleman scholar **Edward Donovan** was the Anglo-Irish traveller, writer and zoologist who was born in Cork in 1768 and who died in 1837.

Founder of the London Museum and Institute of Natural History, he was the author of a number of natural history works, including his *Natural History of British Birds* and natural histories of the insects of both India and China.

Key dates in Ireland's history from the first settlers to the formation of the Irish Republic:

circa 7000 B.C.	Arrival and settlement of Stone Age people.
circa 3000 B.C.	Arrival of settlers of New Stone Age period.
circa 600 B.C.	First arrival of the Celts.
200 A.D.	Establishment of Hill of Tara, Co. Meath, as seat of the High Kings.
circa 432 A.D.	Christian mission of St. Patrick.
800-920 A.D.	Invasion and subsequent settlement of Vikings.
1002 A.D.	Brian Boru recognised as High King.
1014	Brian Boru killed at battle of Clontarf.
1169-1170	Cambro-Norman invasion of the island.
1171	Henry II claims Ireland for the English Crown.
1366	Statutes of Kilkenny ban marriage between native Irish and English.
1529-1536	England's Henry VIII embarks on religious Reformation.
1536	Earl of Kildare rebels against the Crown.
1541	Henry VIII declared King of Ireland.
1558	Accession to English throne of Elizabeth I.
1565	Battle of Affane.
1569-1573	First Desmond Rebellion.
1579-1583	Second Desmond Rebellion.
1594-1603	Nine Years War.
1606	Plantation' of Scottish and English settlers.
1607	Flight of the Earls.
1632-1636	Annals of the Four Masters compiled.
1641	Rebellion over policy of plantation and other grievances.
1649	Beginning of Cromwellian conquest.
1688	Flight into exile in France of Catholic Stuart monarch James II as Protestant Prince William of Orange invited to take throne of England along with his wife, Mary.
1689	William and Mary enthroned as joint monarchs; siege of Derry.
1690	Jacobite forces of James defeated by William at battle of the Boyne (July) and Dublin taken.

1691	Athlone taken by William; Jacobite defeats follow at Aughrim, Galway, and Limerick; conflict ends with Treaty of Limerick (October) and Irish officers allowed to leave for France.
1695	Penal laws introduced to restrict rights of Catholics; banishment of Catholic clergy.
1704	Laws introduced constricting rights of Catholics in landholding and public office.
1728	Franchise removed from Catholics.
1791	Foundation of United Irishmen republican movement.
1796	French invasion force lands in Bantry Bay.
1798	Defeat of Rising in Wexford and death of United Irishmen leaders Wolfe Tone and Lord Edward Fitzgerald.
1800	Act of Union between England and Ireland.
1803	Dublin Rising under Robert Emmet.
1829	Catholics allowed to sit in Parliament.
1845-1849	The Great Hunger: thousands starve to death as potato crop fails and thousands more emigrate.
1856	Phoenix Society founded.
1858	Irish Republican Brotherhood established.
1873	Foundation of Home Rule League.
1893	Foundation of Gaelic League.
1904	Foundation of Irish Reform Association.
1913	Dublin strikes and lockout.
1916	Easter Rising in Dublin and proclamation of an Irish Republic.
1917	Irish Parliament formed after Sinn Fein election victory.
1919-1921	War between Irish Republican Army and British Army.
1922	Irish Free State founded, while six northern counties remain part of United Kingdom as Northern Ireland, or Ulster; civil war up until 1923 between rival republican groups.
1949	Foundation of Irish Republic after all remaining constitutional links with Britain are severed.